Drip, Drip, Drop
EARTH'S WATER

What's So Fresh about Fresh Water?

by Ellen Lawrence

Consultant:

Howard Perlman, Hydrologist

BEARPORT
PUBLISHING

New York, New York

Credits

Cover, © Sharon Day/Shutterstock; 4, © Gorilla Images/Shutterstock; 5TL, © KPG_Payless/Shutterstock; 5TR, © Forster Forest/Shutterstock; 5BL, © Suwan Wanawattanawong/Shutterstock; 5BR, © Wavebreakmedia/Shutterstock; 6, © Dmitry Naumov/Shutterstock; 7, © Aleksandr Ruitin/Shutterstock; 8, © Flo-Bo/Shutterstock; 9, © Four Oaks/Shutterstock; 10T, © Gopfaster/Shutterstock; 10B, © Orla/Shutterstock; 11, © LianeM/Shutterstock; 12, © Creative Travel Projects/Shutterstock; 13, © irin-K/Shutterstock; 14, © Ikunl/Shutterstock; 15, © Xavier Marchant/Shutterstock; 16, © Michal Sarauer/Shutterstock; 17, © Jan Vermeer/Minden Pictures/FLPA; 18, © Zelijko Radojko/Shutterstock; 19, © Sonya Etchison/Shutterstock; 20, © overcrew/Shutterstock; 21L, © Belozorova Elena/Shutterstock; 21C, © Smit/Shutterstock; 21R, © Dmitry Naumov/Shutterstock; 22, © Decha Somparn/Shutterstock, © Sarah2/Shutterstock, and © Gelpi JM/Shutterstock; 23TL, © blackwaterimages/iStock; 23TC, © Michal Sarauer/Shutterstock; 23TR, © Evlakhov Valeriy/Shutterstock; 23BL, © WvdM/Shutterstock; 23BC, © Lenar Musin/Shutterstock; 23BR, © irin-K/Shutterstock.

Publisher: Kenn Goin
Senior Editor: Joyce Tavolacci
Creative Director: Spencer Brinker
Design: Emma Randall
Photo Researcher: Ruby Tuesday Books Ltd

Library of Congress Cataloging-in-Publication Data

Names: Lawrence, Ellen, 1967– author.
Title: What's so fresh about fresh water? / by Ellen Lawrence.
Other titles: What is so fresh about fresh water?
Description: New York, New York : Bearport Publishing, [2016] | Series: Drip, drip, drop: Earth's water | Audience: Ages 7–11._ | Includes bibliographical references and index.
Identifiers: LCCN 2015040047 | ISBN 9781943553235 (library binding) | ISBN 1943553238 (library binding)
Subjects: LCSH: Fresh water—Juvenile literature. | Water-supply—Juvenile literature. | Hydrologic cycle—Juvenile literature.
Classification: LCC GB662.3 .L395 2016 | DDC 551.48—dc23
LC record available at http://lccn.loc.gov/2015040047

For more information, write to Bearport Publishing Company, Inc., 45 West 21st Street, Suite 3B, New York, New York 10010. Printed in the United States of America.

Contents

Water in Our Lives

Every day, we use lots of fresh water.

We splash it on our bodies and brush our teeth with it.

We also drink it and use it for growing food and cooking.

So what exactly is fresh water, and where does it come from?

How many ways do you use water each day? Make a list in a notebook.

4

A person living in the United States uses up to 100 gallons (379 l) of fresh water each day. That's enough water to fill three bathtubs!

5

Fresh or Salty?

There are two main types of water on Earth—salt water and fresh water.

Salt water is found in oceans and seas, and in some lakes.

It contains lots of tiny **particles** of salt that are too small to see.

Fresh water contains fewer salt particles.

It's found in streams, rivers, ponds, and in most lakes.

salty ocean water

Where do you think the salt in salt water comes from?
(The answer is on page 24.)

Only three percent of the water on Earth is fresh water. Lake Baikal in Russia holds more fresh water than any other lake in the world!

Lake Baikal

Why Is Fresh Water Important?

To stay healthy, people need to drink fresh water.

From tiny ants to giant elephants, most animals need fresh water, too.

Trees, grass, and other plants also depend on water for survival.

They take in water from the ground with their roots.

Without fresh water, most animals and plants would die.

If people drink salt water, they become sick. Salt water contains so much salt that it's bad for our bodies.

Earth's Fresh Water

When it rains, fresh water falls from clouds.

The water trickles over the land to form streams and rivers that flow into ponds and lakes.

Some of the rain soaks into the ground.

This underground water is called groundwater.

groundwater

How do you think fresh water gets into clouds?

Snow is made of frozen fresh water. Just like rain, it falls from clouds and lands on the ground. When snow melts, it becomes liquid fresh water.

melting snow

Rain and Snow

How does water become rain?

When water on Earth's surface is warmed by the sun, some of it changes into a **gas**.

The gas, called water vapor, floats high into the sky, where it's cold.

The vapor cools and turns back into tiny droplets of liquid water that form clouds.

Then the water in the clouds falls back down to Earth as rain.

This process is called the **water cycle**.

Sometimes, water vapor in the sky gets so cold that it freezes and makes snowflakes. The snowflakes form clouds and then fall back to Earth.

snowflakes falling

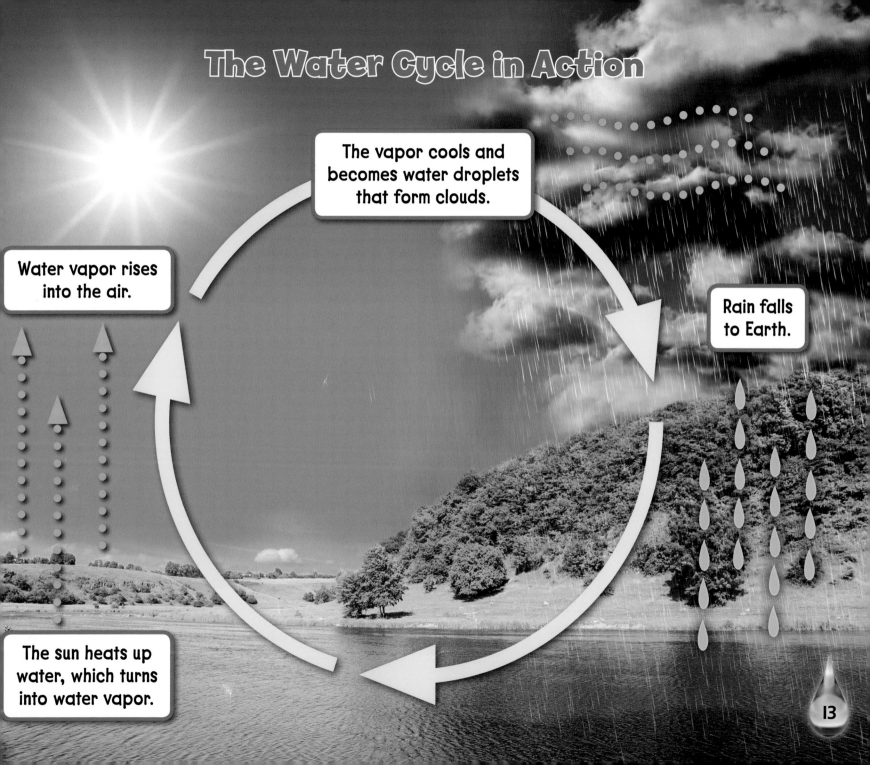

The Water Cycle in Action

The vapor cools and becomes water droplets that form clouds.

Water vapor rises into the air.

Rain falls to Earth.

The sun heats up water, which turns into water vapor.

13

Salt Water into Fresh

Salt water is also part of the water cycle.

When salty ocean water is warmed by the sun, some of it becomes water vapor.

However, the salt particles get left behind in the ocean.

The water vapor cools and becomes raindrops in clouds.

Then the once-salty water falls back to Earth as fresh water!

water vapor

The vapor cools and forms clouds.

Fresh water falls from clouds as rain.

salt water

Salt particles remain in the water.

fresh water in a river

When it rains, fresh water splashes down into salty oceans. Rivers also carry fresh water into oceans. Without this fresh water, oceans would become too salty for fish and other ocean animals to live in.

salt water in the ocean

Frozen Fresh Water

Most of Earth's fresh water is solid ice.

This ice is found in frozen, river-like masses called **glaciers**.

It's also found in giant sheets that cover Greenland and Antarctica.

The ice sheet that stretches across Antarctica is the size of the United States and Mexico combined!

glacier

Snow on mountains, icebergs, and even snowmen in backyards all contain frozen fresh water!

penguins living on an ice sheet in Antarctica

17

Collecting Fresh Water

In many places, people collect and store fresh water in **reservoirs**.

Fresh water flows into reservoirs from rivers.

Water also collects in reservoirs when it rains.

To reach homes and businesses, water from a reservoir travels through miles of pipes.

Then we turn on faucets and fresh water pours out!

reservoir

Sometimes a large amount of fresh water collects underground in one place. This is called an aquifer (AK-wuh-fur). Large pumps bring the groundwater to the surface for people to use.

19

Earth's Precious Water

Only a small amount of Earth's water is liquid fresh water.

So it's important not to **pollute** it with chemicals and trash.

People should also be careful not to waste fresh water.

Without it, people, animals, and plants could not survive.

So let's all take care of Earth's precious fresh water!

a polluted river

Fresh water can become polluted in many ways. Sometimes factories dump waste into rivers and lakes. Some farmers spray chemicals on their fields to kill weeds and insects. These chemicals can then seep into the groundwater.

How many ways can you think of to save water? Make a list in your notebook.
(There are some ideas to get you started on page 24.)

Science Lab

You've discovered that water has three states—liquid, solid, and gas. In this investigation, you will see water's changing states in action.

You will need:
- Water
- A clear plastic cup
- A notebook and a pencil

1. Pour about 0.5 inch (1.3 cm) of water into a plastic cup. Place the cup in a freezer.

   Do you think the water will change? How?

   Write your prediction in your notebook.

2. After two hours, remove the cup from the freezer.

   What do you observe? Does your prediction match what happened?

3. Put the cup in a warm place.

   What do you think will happen next?

   Write your prediction in your notebook.

4. After 30 minutes, check the cup.

   What do you observe inside the cup? Does your prediction match what happened? What do you observe on the outside of the cup? What do you think has happened?

5. Stand the cup in a very warm place, such as a sunny windowsill.

   What do you think will happen to the water now?

   Write your prediction in your notebook.

Science Words

gas (GASS) matter that floats in air and is neither a liquid nor a solid; most gases, such as water vapor, are invisible

glaciers (GLAY-shurz) huge, slow-moving masses of ice that are often about 100 feet (30.5 m) thick

particles (PAR-ti-kuhlz) tiny pieces of something

pollute (puh-LOOT) to release harmful substances into the environment

reservoirs (REZ-ur-vwarz) natural or human-made lakes where fresh water is stored

water cycle (WAH-tur SYE-kuhl) the movement of water from Earth to the sky and then back down again

Index

Read More

Lawrence, Ellen. *Poisoned Rivers and Lakes (Green World, Clean World)*. New York: Bearport (2014).

Nadeau, Isaac. *Water in Glaciers (The Water Cycle)*. New York: Rosen (2003).

Learn More Online

To learn more about fresh water, visit
www.bearportpublishing.com/DripDripDrop

About the Author

Ellen Lawrence lives in the United Kingdom. Her favorite books to write are those about nature and animals. In fact, the first book Ellen bought for herself, when she was six years old, was the story of a gorilla named Patty Cake that was born in New York's Central Park Zoo

Answers

Page 6: The salt in salt water comes from rocks on land that contain tiny particles of salt. When ocean waves break off bits of rocky cliffs or when rivers carry tiny bits of rock into the ocean, salt is carried into the water, too.

Page 21: Here are some ways to save water:

- Never leave the water running when you brush your teeth.
- Take a shower instead of a bath—it uses less water.
- Tell adults not to run the dishwasher until it is completely full.